# A Vague Notion:
## How to Overcome Limiting Beliefs of Fear and Anxiety Through the Word Of God

By: Patrick Baldwin

# Table of Contents

# Invitation

Please Scroll to the Back of the Book for

A Special Gift from God

If You Would Like to Share Your Story
with Us or Stay in Contact Our Contact
Information Can Be Found in the Back
of the Book As Well

Remember . . .

## ~Who You Are In Christ Jesus~

# Dedication

This Book is Dedicated to those struggling to break free from the oppression, lies, fear, and anxiety that the devil attempts to ensnare the Children of God with to discourage them from walking in Faith and Fulfilling their Destiny . . .

God is Waiting Right Now For You To Believe His Word & Take a Step of Faith

Take It Now!

-Resist the Devil & He MUST Flee-

# Forward

If you were to walk through a shopping mall asking people if they believed in God and heaven, a large percentage of people would answer 'yes'. If you asked those same people if they believed in hell and Satan, most would say 'no'.

To put it into 'number form'…

- 76% of people asked believe in heaven
- 71% of people asked believe in hell
- 64% of people asked believe they will go to heaven
- .005% of people asked believe they will go to hell
- 73% of people asked don't believe hell is a real place—that separation from God is just 'out there'

The truth, however, is that Satan and hell are both very real. Both God and Jesus tell us that in no uncertain terms. The Bible also clearly tells us that Satan isn't going anywhere until Jesus returns — that he is actively pursuing anyone and everyone in an effort to pull them away from God. Why? Revenge…plain and simple. Satan lost the battle he waged to overpower God, so he's determined to take as many as possible down with him.

Don't let one of those 'many' be you! Don't fall for Satan's lies. Be encouraged and strengthened by the Word and by the victories of others who have (and still are) lived each day saying "Get behind me, Satan" (Matthew 16:23) you will read in the pages that follow.

# Chapter 1:
# Understanding Your Enemy

### The Devil is Real and He Wants YOU

The devil is mentioned in the Bible early-on; specifically the third chapter of Genesis. Have you ever thought about the fact that God isn't the least bit surprised that Satan shows up? And have you ever thought about the fact that God had declared everything He created on Earth to be "good", yet the devil obviously wasn't good? So what gives?

Here's what 'gives'…Satan was created by God before He created the earth and everyone in it. Satan was created an angel; an angel who decided he was going to elevate himself to be God's equal, or possibly even above God.

This was obviously not well-received by God and resulted in a war between the angles who remained true to God (led by the archangel Michael) and those who sided with Satan (the Bible tells us about one-third of God's angels turned against him).God won (no surprises there); banishing Satan and his followers (demons) from heaven and punishing them with eternal anguish at the time of judgment.

So to answer the questions asked earlier, God wasn't surprised by Satan because his showing up was just another attempt to usurp God's holiness and authority, and because he wasn't created for the earth, everything truly was good.

Okay, so now that you have a little history on who Satan is and how he came to be the way he is, let's get back to the issue at hand; the fact that Satan is real and wants YOU…

The Bible contains numerous incidents involving the devil and his demons including:

- Tempting Jesus following his baptism
- Trying to testify as to who Jesus is through the demon possessed
- Tormenting those who were doing the LORD's work
- Luring people into all sorts of sinful behavior
- Convincing one of Jesus' own disciples to bring about his death

Additionally, the writers of the Bible aren't shy about warning us to be on our guard against the devil and his schemes:

Before we go any farther you need to ask yourself the following question: Do you believe the Bible to be the inspired Word of God? If so, you have to believe every word written — including the verses testifying to the fact that the devil is real and to be feared. Otherwise, you don't truly believe.

For those who believe, the remainder of this book should serve as both a reminder that the devil is real and an encouragement that the power and holiness of God is able to keep you safe from the devil. For those who doubt, the remainder of this book will hopefully convince you of the reality of the devil and persuade you to come to God in repentance, faith, and obedience so that you, too, can find protection from the evil schemes of the devil whose name is Satan.

# Chapter 2: I Can't

Lies the Devil Tells You — I Can't

Satan and his demons have all sorts of tricks 'up their sleeves', but among the most successful in drawing people away from God is the 'trick' lying. The devil never tires of lying. Some of his lies are the in-your-face kind of lies. Examples of these include the lies that say premarital sex being okay, cheating on taxes is as natural as breathing, and that being nice is enough.

Other lies, however, are much subtler. These are the lies that nag at your heart and mess with your mind. These are also the lies that do the most damage because these are the lies that tear away at your confidence and your sense of self-worth. When that happens, you start believing God doesn't love or care about you, so you quit caring about Him, too.

We're going to spend a little time on several of these subtle, yet destructive lies; the first one being the lie that says "I can't".

When God appeared to Moses in the burning bush Moses repeatedly said the words "I can't". He had all sorts of reasons (excuses) he couldn't do what God told him to do; reasons that included not being a good speaker, being too shy, too busy with his sheep and his family, and so on. But God wouldn't have it. He knew what Moses was capable of because He'd made Moses with the intention of having him lead the Israelites to the Promised Land.

Moses had a choice, though. He could have refused to obey. God wouldn't have resorted to taking Moses by the ear and leading him to Egypt. Thankfully Moses allowed God's reasoning and promises to be with him win out over the whisperings of Satan.

You have that same choice. You can either listen to God or to Satan. God doesn't force himself on you the way the devil does. But when you choose God He makes the same promise to you He made to Moses—to never leave you and to tell you what to do and say.

If you are hearing "I can't" you can be sure it's not God's voice you are hearing, but Satan's. So take a deep breath, spend some time in prayer, read Psalms 1, and say "I can...and will delight on the Law of the LORD and meditate on it day and night."

# Chapter 3: It's Not Fair

Lies the Devil Tells You — It's Not Fair

You lost your job. Your spouse was just diagnosed with terminal cancer. Your nine year-old daughter was killed by a drunk driver. Your son was arrested for possession of an illegal substance. Your beloved momma doesn't even know your name or recognize your face anymore. Your spouse cheated on you and wants a divorce. You fill in the blanks with whatever difficulties you've had to face. Now go ahead and say it… "It's not fair!"

It's not fair other people have jobs — especially since you're more deserving, right? It's not fair cancer, dementia, and carelessness bring tragedy to your life! It's not fair other people's kids turn out okay and yours don't. It's not fair your spouse did that to you after all you've put into your marriage! You don't deserve to be treated like this. It's not fair!

Oh, the damage the 'it's not fair' lie can do when it comes to your relationship with God! And yet we keep falling for it time and time again, but the truth of the matter is:

*Life on earth isn't fair and we don't have any right to expect otherwise. That went out the window in the Garden of Eden when none other than the devil himself brought sin into being.

*Everything bad that happens is the result of sin—which is ALL Satan's fault. The sin of greed, stealing, deceit, or a number of other things are almost always the reason businesses fail and jobs are lost. Sexual sins alcoholism, greed, and refusing to listen to God results in failed marriages, killing innocent people, addictions, and all sorts of other things. Cancer and other diseases ARE NOT the result of God zapping us, but they can be the consequence of poor choices we've made (smoking, for instance). Many times, however, they are simply the way our lives are meant to end.

*God never promised fair—He promised his presence, comfort, and strength.
*The ONLY unfair thing to ever happen on Earth was Jesus' death on the cross.

That's right—Jesus is the ONLY person who ever had or ever will have the right to say "Not fair!" Jesus' death was completely and utterly unfair. He did nothing to deserve it other than love us enough to do it so we could have the opportunity to spend eternity with Him and the Father.

Take a minute or two to think about that. Jesus died for no other reason than to make it possible for you to spend eternity with Him in heaven. Are you thinking? Don't let the devil turn you into a whiny child pouting "It's not fair," and asking "Why me?" Instead, look at the cross and into the heart of God and realize the real question is "Why not me?"

# Chapter 4:
# I Don't Have The Time

Lies the Devil Tells You — I Don't Have Time

Noah could have said he didn't have time to build the ark that saved his lives, the lives of his family, and served to preserve the human race. Peter, Andrew, James, and John could have said they didn't have time to follow Jesus when He told them to leave their nets and their boats to be fishers of men. Jesus could have said He didn't have time to mess with the crowd instead of feeding them with the loaves and fish in one boy's lunch box. Jesus could also say He doesn't have time to listen to desperate prayers of people who haven't paid any attention to Him in years (if ever) or to 'mess' with putting people and situations in our lives that serve to keep us from messing up big time. But they didn't, Jesus doesn't, and neither should we.

Satan fills our heads with all sorts of excuses (we call them reasons) for not having time to give to Jesus. We need to work. We need the overtime. Sunday is the only day I can sleep in. The kids want to play on this or that team and it's not your fault they play on Sunday. I'm tired. The yard needs to be mowed. If I volunteer for that I won't be able to…. Those people don't deserve or appreciate what you do for them so why should I waste my time on them when I could be…. The kid would rather have the stuff my time away from home buys them more than they want me around.

The devil wants you to believe you don't have time to give your family what they really want and need (time). He wants you to believe your time is too precious and limited to give to worship God and to serve Him by serving others. He wants you to believe your time is yours and that giving God any of it is a waste of time and energy; that your time would be better spent doing anything other than 'God stuff'. Lies, lies, and more lies!

I know it's easy to fall for lies like this, given the fact that we live such busy, hectic lives, but the truth of the matter is that we have time for the things we want to have time for. Cindy, a sweet and dedicated Christian, wife, and mom was reminded of this by her husband one day—a day she said changed her perspective from that day forward…

*Curt and I had been happily married for many years when he opened my eyes big time to how Satan uses even the best things to trip us up. One evening he asked me to go fishing with him the next day – just the two of us. I'm not so big on fishing, but spending the day enjoying the sun on the boat is usually appealing, but I wasn't in the mood to do so, so I said no – that I had too much to do. A couple of hours later a young lady who had been in my youth group at church for several years, called and asked if she could come over the next day to talk. I was just about to say sure, come on over, when I saw Curt watching me. He could tell from my end of the conversation what Ellen wanted, and the hurt in his eyes was unnerving. I told Ellen I'd call her back in a few minutes and let her know and hung up the phone. Curt simply looked at me and said, "Do you really have time for Ellen but not for me? I mean, I get that most of those kids are still really connected to you and I respect that a lot, but…well, it hurts to think that…." He didn't finish. He didn't have to. I called Ellen, told her I'd have more time for her in a couple of days because I was spending the next day with Curt. Satan tried to make me believe spending time with my husband was a waste of time – that nurturing our marriage wasn't important. But it is. It's important to God and to Curt and me.*

Remember…you have time for the things you want to have time for. This means the key to not being susceptible to this lie is prioritizing your life by *wanting* to have time for God and everything he holds dear.

# Chapter 5:
# I Don't Have The Money

Lies the Devil Tells You — I Don't Have the
Money

The Bible records an incident in which Jesus and
the disciples are in the temple and happen to see
others coming in and giving their offering.
Among those who do so are a rich man and a
poor widow woman. The rich man puts in some
money and goes on about the business of
worshipping. The poor widow woman also puts
money in — two coins that were literally all she
had (Luke 21:1-3).

Jesus quickly points out to his disciples that even
though the rich man gave more from a
quantitative viewpoint, it was the widow
woman who gave the greater amount because
she gave sacrificially — meaning she gave even
though it would leave her at a 'loss' to provide
for herself.

Notice the '' around the word loss. They're there because she wasn't really at a loss. She was fine because of her faith—faith that told her God would bless her generous and sacrificial gift by providing for her needs. This woman had no room in her heart or her mind for the devil's lie that says we don't have the money to give to the church, missionaries, or to those in need. She didn't believe the devil when he undoubtedly whispered things in her ear like: "They need to be giving you money instead of you giving it to them." "If you think you're going to get anything out of this, you're wrong!"

"I bet you'll be sorry you did that when you're hungry and no one bothers to help you."

When it comes to giving—your money, time, or talents—God has quite a bit to say on the subject and makes quite a few promises in regards to how he deals with our giving. Let's look at a few of them now…

*Every man shall give as he is able, according to the blessing of the Lord your God that he has given you. ~Deuteronomy 16:17*

*Each one must give as he has decided in his heart, not reluctantly or under compulsion, for God loves a cheerful giver. ~2nd Corinthians 9:7*

*Bring the full tithe into the storehouse, that there may be food in my house. And thereby put me to the test, says the Lord of hosts, if I will not open the windows of heaven for you and pour down for you a blessing until there is no more need. ~Malachi 3:10*

*And he said to them, "Take care, and be on your guard against all covetousness, for one's life does not consist in the abundance of his possessions." ~Luke 12:15*

When talking about holding on to what we have vs. giving to God, there are a few things everyone needs to understand in order to be able to give with a cheerful heart and to give *knowing* God will supply your needs.

#1: Everything we have is God's to begin with. Your money, your house, your job, your children, your spouse, your ability to see things through the lens of a camera like no one else can, or your aptitude for trivia…it's all a gift from God. So to give to God is, in actuality, giving *back* to God.

#2: Giving is an act of faith and faith never goes unnoticed or is unappreciated by God. A parent provides for a child out of love and acknowledges and rewards a child for their obedience. God does the same because he is our Father…and he does it better.

#3: God never makes a promise he doesn't keep. He has promised to supply our every need when we put our faith in him…and he will.

Don't let the devil rob you of enjoying the joy and peace of mind that comes when you give and the emotional and spiritual blessings that come from seeing God work in your life.

# Chapter 6: It's Okay

Lies the Devil Tells You — It's Okay

Of all the lies Satan tells, this one is the one we are most gullible to. Think about it...

- In less than fifty years we've gone from TV's married couples sleeping in twin beds to unmarried couples sleeping together and having sex on the scene

- Pregnant teens are celebrated

- Harmful and addictive drugs are legal

- Suggestive clothes are considered cute and fashionable on ten year-olds

- Churches are accepting homosexuality as okay

- The divorce rate among those who say they are Christians is no lower than it is for non-Christians

- Nativity scenes, religious Christmas carols, and prayer in public venues are rarely allowed

- The devil started with the 'little' things — dress codes, cuss words, and leaving something to the imagination on the big (and little) screen. These things were a choice. You didn't have to wear, say, or watch. But once the majority of people were wearing, saying, and watching without bursting into flames, the 'okay-ness' of these things found their way into the Church and the homes of dedicated Christians. If you've been raised in the Church or are over the age of fifty, you'll know what I mean when I say this: If you don't believe this is true, think about the upheaval over women wearing pants to church.

The devil was rubbing his hands together in glee over his success, but being…well, the devil, he wasn't satisfied. He kept going. A little here and a little there, chipping away at the overall morality of society until he brought us to where we are today…a sinful, immoral society in which even many Christians are refusing to draw the line in the sand between right and wrong.

"It's okay", people say. "It's okay for people to live the way they see fit." "It's okay to excuse that sin because the majority of people want to."

But it's NOT okay. It's not okay because God says it isn't okay. God hasn't changed His views on sin or what is and isn't sin. He hasn't ordered a re-write of the Bible. So when your head and your heart say it's okay, check your sources. If the Bible doesn't say it's okay then it's not. Plain and simple; leaving you with the decision to listen to God or to Satan. My prayer is that you choose God.

# Chapter 7: It's No Use

Lies the Devil Tells You — It's No Use

In spite of being raised in a loving home with discipline and guidance, Danny chose to go in the opposite direction — a direction that led to a failed marriage, a little boy who wouldn't know his dad, and spending a few years in prison.

A lot of people in Danny's shoes only go from bad to worse once they've gone this far for one reason and one reason only: they believe the 'it's no use' lie the devil plays over and over in their head and speaks through other people (parents, parole officers, peers, and people in society who won't look beyond your past). Thankfully, however, Danny didn't listen to those voices. Instead, Danny listened to the prison chaplain and to his heart.

Danny's grandmother, who had always been his biggest fan and encourager, died shortly before he went to prison. He was allowed to see her before she passed; allowed to hear her tell him he was better than he was allowing himself to be. She told him she loved him but hoped this wasn't the final goodbye for them — that he would find his way to the LORD so that she would see him again someday.

In the beginning this only made Danny angrier and more self-destructive, but out of boredom, desperation, or possibly even a push from God, Danny went to a Bible study held each week in the prison led by a young preacher not much older than Danny. The two initially connected over their shared 'love' for the St. Louis Cardinals but before long Danny was actually listening to what the preacher had to say and didn't object when he asked Danny if he could pray for him.

Six months before Danny was released he was baptized into Christ. Today he is preaching full-time, married to a loving and supportive wife, has a beautiful baby girl, and has asked his first wife's forgiveness for the pain he caused her and their son. To date she has refused his efforts to make amends, but Danny says he will just keep praying and trying. He didn't listen to the devil's 'it's no use' lie about his future before and he refuses to do so now.

As long as you are breathing and your heart is beating, there is hope for you to know and experience the mercy, forgiveness, love, and blessings God has in mind for you. The lie that 'it's no use' is just that—a line. You are precious in God's sight. You do matter and He does have a use for you.

# Chapter 8:
# I'm A Failure

Lies the Devil Tells You — I'm a Failure

What is failure? Failure is giving up. Failure is NOT making mistakes. Failure is NOT losing. Failure is NOT getting it wrong. Failure is giving up…having a defeatist attitude…falling for the devil's lie that your self-worth is zilch.

When Samson woke to find his hair and strength gone and that he had been deceived by his wife, he believed for a while that he had failed. But when he was pushed to the limits his faith was renewed and he asked God to work in him one final time. He didn't want his life to end before he did one last thing to proclaim God's holiness.

When Peter heard that rooster crow early in the morning following Jesus' arrest, you know he had to feel like a complete and utter failure. The devil was surely rubbing his hands together in glee and doing a little victory dance, but he was a bit premature. Peter's love for the Savior and determination to make things right was bigger than the part of him who listened to the devil's lies labeling Peter a failure.

Samson and Peter are just two examples of what it means to reject the devil's lies that say you are a failure. They messed up. They made mistakes. They sinned. They regrouped, though, by owning their mistakes, righting their wrongs, and looking deep into the eyes and heart of Jesus for direction and assurance.

And then there's Judas Iscariot the betrayer. Judas was with Jesus like Peter was. He witnessed the miracles. He heard the words of teaching, admonishment, and promise. He experienced the companionship of Jesus. He knew Jesus as a man of compassion and giver of second chances, but it wasn't enough. When Judas fully realized what he had done in betraying Jesus, he believed the devil's message of failure playing over and over again in his head. Judas believed his actions to be a complete and utter failure without any chance of forgiveness and he gave up. He committed suicide; taking away any and every chance he had for making things right between him and God.

Christian author, Darla Noble, says "God promises that in the end everything will be okay, so if things aren't okay, it's not the end." So hang in there and keep trying. Lay your mistakes and poor choices at the feet of Jesus and say "I need you to help me get this right" and tell Satan to get lost because you aren't giving up.

# Chapter 9:
# I Don't Deserve It

Lies the Devil Tells You — I'm not Good Enough
and Don't Deserve It

Joseph was a somewhat cocky teenager God sent
to Egypt (under less-than-desirable
circumstances). He hadn't been there too terribly
long before being falsely accused of rape, which
led to serving a lengthy prison sentence. While
in prison, however, Joseph became aware of the
fact that God was actively working in his life by
allowing him to interpret dreams. This
eventually led to Joseph's release from prison so
that he could interpret a dream for the Pharaoh,
and *this* led to Joseph being in charge of the
entire nation of Egypt…which allowed him to
bring his father (Jacob) along with all his
brothers and their families to Egypt so they
wouldn't starve during a horrible drought.
It would have been easy for Joseph to plead 'not
good enough' when Pharaoh wanted to elevate
him to position of great leadership, but he
didn't.

Paul, previously known as Saul, would have had a solid case for not being good enough to take the message of the Gospel to people all over the known world. After all, he'd been a Christian-killer (and one with gusto, I might add).

Rita grew up in an abusive home. From there she became an abused wife. It wasn't until her husband started to abuse their two year-old daughter, however, that she finally found the courage to leave. It wasn't easy, but with the help of the staff at a safe-shelter and a church family who took her into their loving care and fellowship, she did it. She and her daughter were able to start over, and for the first time in her life, Rita knew what it meant to be happy. Two years later she met a man at church who asked her on a date. It took a while, but she finally agreed to go. Almost a year after that first date, Michael asked Rita and her daughter to become his wife and daughter. Rita resisted because she didn't feel good enough to be anyone's wife. She didn't deserve to be loved that way…by a good man…did she?

The devil would love to make you think you aren't good enough, either. It's one of his favorite 'tricks' to keep you from resting in God's comfort and becoming the person God created you to be. The devil thrives on tearing down our self-esteem, because when he does *that,* he is able to make us believe God doesn't care about us—that we aren't good enough to be on His radar list. But guess what? Nothing could be farther from the truth! God created you with as much TLC as you hold your newborn baby. He created each of us with specific purposes in mind; meaning He sees each of us as valued and cherished.

To put it as simply as possible, God has 20/20 vision when it comes to His creation. He knows our worth because He created us. If you believe otherwise, it's because you are looking at yourself through the devil's perspective. So take a good long look at yourself in the mirror and see the real you—the real and wonderful you God created that is good enough to do anything He wants you to do.

# Chapter 10:
# No One Cares

Lies the Devil Tells You — No One Cares

Another one of the devil's lies is the one that says no one cares. No one? Not one single person? That's what he'd like you to believe, and unfortunately, he's been quite successful.

Depression, addictions and dependencies on alcohol, drugs, sex, porn, gambling, and even food are all outward displays of the belief that no one cares about you. Trying to buy people's acceptance and affection with expensive gifts is proof you believe these things are necessary in order to be loved and cared for. Being a people-pleaser at all costs — including being someone you aren't in order to meet their expectations — is proof you believe no one cares about the real you.

When you do these things — when you let the devil's lies control your 'take' on what you bring to a relationship — you are cheating both yourself and others. You are cheating yourself out of the joy that comes from being in healthy relationships. Relationships between family and friends are one of God's gifts to us. He created us to be social because He is social.

Other people lose out too, with your nobody-likes-me-everybody-hates-me attitude. In closing yourself off from others you cheat them out of knowing the really great person you are and out of being socially responsible (showing compassion, nurturing you, etc.).

Kimberly's life is a prime example of this. She was always a bit shy, but still enjoyed positive relationships with her family and a few close friends. She never had a boyfriend in high school, though. She was too shy. Instead, she just admired the boys from afar. But when she was twenty, a guy at work asked her out and she said yes.

The first date led to a second and a third and before she knew it, they had been going out for nearly six months. She was really beginning to have feelings for him and was beyond thankful he hadn't pressured her for sex; something she wasn't anywhere near ready for. Sadly, the relationship ended when Kimberly and her older sisters went out to celebrate the youngest sister's birthday. They were just leaving the restaurant when in walks Kimberly's boyfriend with another girl who was obviously not his sister.

Too shy and too heartbroken to say anything, she simply left. He called her late that night, apologized for leading her on; explaining he and the girl she'd seen him with were deeply in love, but that they'd agreed to take a break from one another to see if it really was the 'real thing'. Kimberly is now fifty-four years old. She never dated again because she was convinced no man would ever really and truly care about her the way she wanted him to.

The Bible gives us a few examples of people who have the same attitude. Elijah is one of those people. King Ahab and Queen Jezebel were after him like syrup on pancakes. Elijah, who was a prophet, wasn't the least bit shy when it came to letting the king and queen know God was not pleased with them, and they didn't like that. In fact, they hated it to the point of wanting Elijah dead.

Elijah whined and moaned to God, saying nobody cared about him and that he was the only person in the entire kingdom who lived in obedience to God. A loose paraphrase of what God told Elijah is this: Quit whining, because you're not the only person, but even if you were it wouldn't matter because I'm here, I care, and I will take care of you.

Do you see where I'm going with this? I hope so, but just in case…

Someone does care about you. In fact, there are most likely several someones who care and who care deeply. But even if you don't believe that or can't find those people, it's okay because God is there, He cares, and He's not going anywhere.

# Chapter 11:
# No Chance For The Devil

The Devil Doesn't Have a Chance When You Let
God Take Control

The difficult situations we face in everyday life
such as disagreements with co-workers, financial
problems, a less-than-honest landlord, or pesky
telemarketers that won't take no for an answer,
are easy enough to deal with because they are
tangible issues, so to speak. We can see them,
talk to them, touch them…. But when it comes to
emotional and spiritual struggles resulting from
the lies

Satan bombards us with day after day after day,
well, it's not always easy, is it? In fact, it is
downright impossible to do on our own. The
only way we can successfully deal with the devil
and make sure we come out the winner is to let
God take control. The word control is somewhat
scary to many — especially when it means
handing control of your life over to someone
else. But it doesn't have to be scary if the one
you are handing yourself over to is the very one
who made you…Father God.

Think of it like this: Who would you rather have watch your baby while you and your husband enjoy a well-deserved evening alone—your mother or your three year-old? I know! I know! Your mother, right? She has the experience, the maturity, the wisdom, the ability, and the love your baby needs. Your three year-old possibly has enough love, but other than that and some stuffed toys or building blocks....

The point I'm trying to make is that handing control of your life over to God makes perfect sense because He is the Creator, the Almighty, the LORD of lords. He knows you best, He knows what is best for you, and most importantly, He has the power necessary to undermine and toss aside any scheme or lie the devil plants in your mind or in your path.

God is bigger than any lie Satan tells. God is bigger than any hurt you experience because of Satan's lies. God is big enough to see you through it all.

# Chapter 12: Conclusion

Throughout this book there has been much said to encourage you to take a step of faith and believe God's Word to be true. Ultimately, however, this decision is up to you – Are you going to believe God's Word or the lies of this World? Who's report will you believe God's or the Devil's – Seems like an easy choice right?

Well only if you're following God in all truth and sincerity. Getting in His Word is the first step to overcoming your limiting beliefs of fear and anxiety. If you are suffering from depression as well I highly suggest you read the book of Psalms continually – and yes it helps with fear & anxiety as well.

Start out step by step – it doesn't have to be a big step but it does have to be in faith. Immerse yourself in the Word of God, Prayer, and Worship each and every day to fight back against these lies that cause limiting beliefs.

Remember we are all in a spiritual war – You can either live a victorious life through the power of God or Not – God has given you the power to chose. You know He wants the best for His Children – Trust Him Now and Start Reading the Book of Psalms.

# A Special Gift

*God has a Gift for You!*

## Plan of Salvation:

There is no formal " prayer of salvation" as many churches would have you believe, God's word is very clear – there is only one way to get to the Father in heaven and that is through Jesus Christ (John 14:6).  Jesus says that you must be born again to enter into heaven (John 3:3-5).

Salvation is simply the first step in building an open & honest relationship with God.  We all have sinned and fall short every day, but there is Hope in Jesus Christ – Just cry out to God in sincerity and honesty for forgiveness asking Him to Save you, Sanctify you, and fill you with His Holy Spirit – Ask for His will to be done in your life on earth as it is in Heaven – That's it, now just keep it real with God.

## A Warning:

The Christian walk is not an easy life on the surface. The word of God says that we will be hated in all the world for Christ namesake (Matt. 24:9). The Bible says that in the last days are enemy prevail against us until Christ returns to save us (Dan 7:21, 22). Furthermore, we must endure hardship as a good soldier of Jesus Christ (2 Tim 2:3) – yet we are never alone in this, God promises us that He will never leave us nor forsake us if we believe in him (Matt.28:20).

In everything we go through we have the peace & joy of God which surpasses all understanding (Philp. 4:6-8) The Bible declares, "For I consider the sufferings of this present time are not worthy to be compared with the glory which shall be revealed in us. (Rom 8:18). However, in all these things we are more than conquerors through Jesus Christ (Rom. 8:37)

# Contact Information

## Our Contact Information

Stay in Contact with the American Christian
Defense Alliance, Inc

# Contactus@acdainc.org

# Or

# Email Us Though
# Our Website At:
# http://acdainc.org

Visit Our Friend **Darla Noble** as well – She is a great
Christian author with books I'm sure you'll love

# Join Our Mailing List

We also Greatly Appreciate You Signing Up For Our Mailing List and Providing a Good Rating for This Book.

If You or Your Family have been Blessed by this book please let us know by dropping us a line through our website at **http://acdainc.org**

Thanks Again for Reading

God Bless!

# Get All Our Books:

### Click the Link Below:

# Check Out All The American Christian Defense Alliance, Inc. Books On Amazon

www.ingramcontent.com/pod-product-compliance
Lightning Source LLC
Chambersburg PA
CBHW021920040426
42448CB00007B/843